Great Minds of Science

Carl Linnaeus

Father of Classification

Revised Edition

Margaret J. Anderson

Enslow Publishers, Inc.
40 Industrial Road
Box 398
Berkeley Heights, NJ 07922
USA

http://www.enslow.com

Library of Congress Cataloging-in-Publication Data

Anderson, Margaret Jean, 1931–
    Carl Linnaeus : father of classification / Margaret J. Anderson. — Rev. ed.
        p. cm. — (Great minds of science)
    Includes bibliographical references and index.
    Summary: "A biography of eighteenth-century Swedish botanist Carl Linnaeus, who established the modern system of classifying plants and animals"—Provided by publisher.
        ISBN-13: 978-0-7660-3009-1
        ISBN-10: 0-7660-3009-1
    1. Linné, Carl von, 1707–1778—Juvenile literature. 2. Naturalists—Sweden—Biography—Juvenile literature. I. Title.
    QH44.A63 2009
    580.92—dc22
        [B]   2008023941

Printed in the United States of America

10 9 8 7 6 5 4 3 2 1

To Our Readers: We have done our best to make sure all Internet Addresses in this book were active and appropriate when we went to press. However, the author and the publisher have no control over and assume no liability for the material available on those Internet sites or on other Web sites they may link to. Any comments or suggestions can be sent by e-mail to comments@enslow.com or to the address on the back cover.

♻ Enslow Publishers, Inc., is committed to printing our books on recycled paper. The paper in every book contains 10% to 30% post-consumer waste (PCW). The cover board on the outside of each book contains 100% PCW. Our goal is to do our part to help young people and the environment too!

Illustration Credits: C. Y. Li, pp. 45, 59 ; Cary Kerst, p. 67; Courtland Smith, pp. 32, 73; Enslow Publishers, Inc., pp. 12, 41; The Granger Collection, New York, pp. 36, 75; Margaret J. Anderson, pp. 10, 11, 15, 18, 20, 23, 28, 38, 47, 55, 63, 65, 77, 79, 84, 92, 103, 104; Mary Evans Picture Library/Everett Collection, p. 89; Niels Quist/Shutterstock Images LLC, p. 69; Serge Lamere/Shutterstock Images LLC, p. 94; Stephen J. Delisle/Enslow Publishers, Inc., p. 30.

Cover Illustration: Margaret J. Anderson (foreground); Jupiterimages Corporation/ Photos.com (background).

Contents

Pronunciation of Swedish Names

Many Swedish words may appear hard to pronounce, but they can often be sounded out. For example, Stenbrohult is pronounced Sten-bro-hult. Vowels with an accent mark mean the sound of the vowel is changed. Here is a short guide to some of the vowel sounds:

å—Sounds like the "o" in "hope." (Example: Umeå is pronounced Um-e-oh.)

ö—Pronounced by saying "ah" with rounded lips. (Example: Öland is pronounced oe-land.)

ä—Sounds like the "e" in "bet" or "met." (Example: Växjö is a hard name to say. It is pronounced vek-yhoe.)

A Passion for Names

On May 23, 2007, an American professor of botany threw a birthday party for Carl Linnaeus. The room was decked out with flowers. Long tables were covered with heaping bowls of food. There was a cake, of course. The only thing missing was the guest of honor. This did not surprise anyone. Linnaeus was long dead. The guests had gathered to celebrate his three-hundredth birthday!

The food was mostly salads and grains, except for a platter of frog's legs. Beside each plate was a recipe listing the ingredients. The names were in Latin: a salad that featured *Oryza sativa*, *Pisum sativum*, *Cucumis sativus*, *Helianthus annuus*—rice, peas, cucumber, and sunflower seeds; a side dish of fried *Bombyx mori*—

sillkworm pupae; and legs of *Rana tigrina*. Each Latin name was followed by the letter *L*, which stood for Linnaeus. All the ingredients in the foods at the party had been named by Linnaeus. His claim to fame is that he worked out a system for naming all the plants and animals that fill our world. This was a huge job. Linnaeus himself remarked that it "demanded time and almost did away with sleep."[1]

Two-Word Names

Before Linnaeus took on the task of organizing the plant and animal kingdoms, names were mostly long strings of words. Linnaeus gave each kind of plant and animal just two names. The first name told the genus (group) to which the plant or animal belonged. The second name described the species within that group. This two-word system of naming is known as the binomial system of nomenclature.

We sometimes use a two-word system in naming everyday objects. For example, we speak of carving knives, dinner knives, steak knives, pocket knives, and hunting knives. These are all different kinds of knives. The first part of each knife's name tells us what type of knife it is. Linnaeus's system worked the same way, but he wrote in Latin because that was the language of science. In Latin, the noun is placed before the adjective, so the group name comes first. Related types of plants or animals share the same group or *first* name. The *second* word, or species, is an adjective that describes a special characteristic.

Let us take a closer look at an example of binomial naming. Linnaeus called white clover *Trifolium repens*. *Trifolium* means "three leaves," which comes from the typical clover shape of the plant's leaves. *Repens* means "creeping." The plant grows or creeps close to the ground. Crimson clover is called *Trifolium incarnatum*. *Incarnatum* means "blood red." White and crimson clover share the same first name. They are both kinds of clover. They belong to the same group or genus. In botany books, the names are followed by the letter *L*. That tells us that Linnaeus named them.

The Language of Science

Although Latin is no longer spoken, giving plants and animals Latin names has worked out well. It means that the scientific name, in contrast to the common name, is the same in every language. Common names, such as white clover, often vary from place to place, even where the same language is spoken. Linnaeus's own name is a good example.[2] It comes from the Swedish word *linn*, which means "linden tree." In Britain, the linden is known as the lime tree, although it has nothing to do with the tree that grows the lime fruit. In some parts of North America, the linden is called basswood; in other places it is the whitewood tree. However, the tree's Latin genus name, *Tilia*, is the same everywhere.

If Linnaeus wanted to name a plant using a word that did not exist in Latin, he simply added a Latin ending. For example, Linnaeus called the tobacco plant *Nicotiana tabacum*. He named the genus *Nicotiana* after Jean Nicot, who introduced tobacco farming in France. The species name is from an American Indian name for the tobacco plant.

The naming and classifying of plants and animals is called taxonomy. Two seventeenth-century taxonomists laid the foundation for Linnaeus's important work. One was John Ray, an Englishman. He based his system of classifying plants on several features—fruits, flowers, and leaves. Joseph Tournefort, a French botanist, looked only at the shape of the petals. Linnaeus divided plants into different classes based on the number and position of the stamens, the male part of the flower. His was an easier system to describe and to use.

Linnaeus named so many plants and animals that he has been called "God's Registrar."[3] The number of times *L.* appears after a scientific name shows how hard he worked at naming things. He often honored his friends by naming plants after them. However, only one flower

Linnaea borealis is the only plant named after Linnaeus. The common name for this plant is twinflower.

bears his name. *Linnaea borealis*, the twinflower, was his favorite plant. He loved to see its delicate pink blossoms on the forest floor in early summer.

A New Twig on the Family Tree

Carl Linnaeus was born in a simple, turf-roofed house in Råshult in the south of Sweden. His father, Nils, had built the house for his bride, Christina. Nils loved flowers. Next to their home, he had planted an unusual border. The shrubs were arranged like guests around a dinner table covered with flowers. He used to decorate baby Carl's crib with blossoms.

Christina was the daughter of the pastor in the nearby village of Stenbrohult. Nils was his assistant. In 1708, a year after Carl was born, Christina's father died. Nils became senior pastor and the family moved into Christina's old home next to the church.

Nils Linnaeus built this turf-roofed house for his bride Christina, in Råshult, Sweden. This house became the birthplace of Carl Linnaeus.

When Linnaeus was born, Sweden was one of the most powerful nations in Europe. After several disastrous wars against Russia, however, Sweden lost most of its influence.

Later, Carl described the setting as "one of the most beautiful places in all Sweden, for it lies on the shores of the big lake of Möckeln. . . . [It] is surrounded on all sides by flat arable land, except to the west where it is lapped by the clear waters of the lake. Away to the south are lovely beech woods, to the north the high mountain ridge of Taxås."[4]

One sunny afternoon, when Carl was about four, the Linnaeus family and some friends went on a picnic by the lake. They gathered bunches of wildflowers. Nils told his guests what each flower was called. After that, Carl wanted to know the name of every plant in the garden and nearby fields. The little boy had a hard time remembering the long strings of Latin words. He asked his father to repeat them again and again. Nils told the child sharply that he was not going to tell him names just to have them forgotten. From then on, Carl concentrated on learning them. Naming plants became his lifelong passion.

The Reluctant Student

CHRISTINA LINNAEA HOPED THAT CARL WOULD BE a pastor like his father and his grandfather before him. When he was seven, Carl's parents hired a tutor. But young Carl did not like to study. He would much rather be out in the garden among the flowers than indoors reading. His father, Nils Linnaeus, often took Carl's side when his mother scolded. In his autobiography, Carl Linnaeus later described his father as being "very gentle, calm, and kindly." His mother, on the other hand, was "shrewd, lively, and diligent."[1]

Two years later, Nils finally agreed that the boy needed to study harder. Carl was sent off to school in Växjö, a country town about thirty miles away. He found it hard to say goodbye to

These are deep purple and white hollyhocks. They come in many other colors as well. Nils gave his son flowers to play with from a very early age, fostering Carl's interest in botany.

the places he loved—the lake, the fields, and the garden. It was also hard to leave his parents and his three younger sisters. The following year, a little brother was born.

The teachers in Växjö had no more luck turning young Carl into a scholar than had his tutor. Carl found schooldays long and boring. Classes began at 6 A.M. and lasted until 5 P.M. Most of that time was spent learning Latin and Greek, or studying the Bible. The teachers were so severe that they made the students' "hair stand on end."[2]

Carl was still interested in plants. Sometimes he went off looking for flowers instead of attending class. Although he was popular with the other students, he liked to be alone. They nicknamed him "the little botanist."[3]

In high school, Carl still considered most classes a waste of time. Greek and Hebrew were aimed at students who wanted to be pastors. However, Carl did enjoy logic and physics. They were taught by Johan Rothman, the town doctor. Dr. Rothman took a liking to Carl.

He encouraged him and lent him books. He told Carl that botany would be a good field of study for him.

Nils Visits Växjö

Toward the end of Carl's school years, Nils Linnaeus was worried about his health. He decided to go to Växjö to consult Dr. Rothman. While he was in town, he checked up on how Carl was doing in school. The teachers' answers must have come as a shock. They told Nils that his son was a hopeless student. He had no chance of becoming a pastor. He would be better off learning a trade. He might make a good shoemaker, but he would never be a clergyman.

Poor Nils! All the money he spent on Carl's education had been wasted! How was he going to break the news to Christina? Feeling very downcast, he went to see Dr. Rothman. After they had talked about his own health, Nils asked the doctor's advice on what to do about Carl.

This time the answer was more encouraging. Rothman agreed with the other teachers that

Nils Linnaeus (shown here) was upset when he learned that Carl was not suited to be a pastor. However, Dr. Rothman felt that Carl would be better off if he tried to further his interest in plants.

Carl would never be a clergyman, but he did not think he should be a shoemaker. He suggested that Carl should be a doctor. The boy's keen interest in plants would carry him a long way. Medical students needed a thorough knowledge of botany. At that time, almost all medicines were made from plants.

Nils Linnaeus was not completely convinced. Christina would be unhappy that their plans for Carl's career were not working out. At that time, a pastor's job was more secure than a doctor's. Should they be spending still more money on Carl's education when there were the younger children to worry about?

Dr. Rothman came up with a generous offer. He said that Carl could live with him for the next year. Carl would be his private student until he was ready to go to university.

The plan worked well. The doctor taught Carl anatomy and physiology. He also introduced him to Tournefort's method of classifying plants by the shape of their petals. At the end of the school year, when Carl returned

Christina Linnaea is pictured here in her wedding gown. She, too, was not pleased when she learned that Carl would not become a pastor as she had hoped.

to Stenbrohult, he spent the long summer days studying flowers. He worked on his plant collection. He followed Tournefort's method of classification. Sometimes it worked. Sometimes it did not.

Lund University

In August 1727, Carl enrolled at Lund University. It seemed a good choice. His father had studied there and a family friend was dean of its cathedral. Unfortunately, Carl got off to a poor start. As he rode into town, all the bells were tolling. When he asked someone the reason, he learned that the dean had just died. In addition, Carl did not like what he could see of Lund. Geese and pigs wandered up and down the dirty streets, rooting through the filth and garbage.

The university turned out to be no more promising than the town. Only one professor lectured in medicine. No one taught botany.

Linnaeus rented a room from Dr. Stobaeus, Lund's leading doctor. Stobaeus was interested in natural history. He had his own museum of birds, plants, rocks, and shells. He also had a large collection of dried plants, called an herbarium, and a good library.

To escape from the dreary town, Linnaeus often went out into the countryside looking for plants. He explored the meadows and flat salt marshes. There he found plants that did not grow in the rolling hills around Stenbrohult. He noticed that different types of plants grow in different types of surroundings. He was eager to know the names of these unfamiliar plants. The books in the doctor's library had the answers, but the library was always kept locked.

The doctor's secretary, who was a fellow student, had a key to the library. He and Linnaeus were good friends. He agreed to sneak books out of the library for Linnaeus. In return, Linnaeus promised to help him with his physiology homework.

Linnaeus stayed up late, poring over the borrowed books by candlelight. The doctor's elderly mother slept in a nearby room. Night

After high school, Linnaeus continued his education at Lund University. Often, he could be found up late at night reading books from Dr. Stobaeus's library.

after night, she saw a light shining in Carl's room. She thought that the careless young man had the habit of falling asleep with a candle still burning. The house was old and was built of wood. An open flame could easily start a fire. Finally, she spoke to Dr. Stobaeus about her fears.

At two o'clock the following morning the doctor burst into Linnaeus's room. He expected to find Carl sleeping. Instead, he was sitting at a table surrounded by a pile of books. When the doctor realized that they were books from *his* locked library, he demanded an explanation. He listened in silence to what Linnaeus had to say. Then he ordered him to put out the light and go to bed. They would talk again in the morning.

The next day, the interview went far better than Linnaeus had dared to hope. The doctor questioned him about his interest in botany. When he found out how serious Linnaeus was about studying plants, he gave Linnaeus the run of the library. He even offered him a free room and meals.

Linnaeus returned to Stenbrohult for the summer. One day, Dr. Rothman came over to visit. On hearing that botany was not taught at Lund, he advised Carl to transfer to Uppsala University. Uppsala was 250 miles (400 kilometers) away. Carl's father agreed to the change. But when he handed his son money for the journey, he said that this was all the financial help Carl could expect from his parents. From then on, he would be on his own.

Uppsala University

UPPSALA WAS BUILT ON THE WEST BANK OF THE Fyris River. A huge castle and a red-brick cathedral dominated the city. The university, founded in 1477, was the oldest in Sweden. Today it is a leading university, but when Linnaeus enrolled, Uppsala University was going through bad times.

Uppsala had twice as many professors of medicine as Lund had—two! One of these old men, Olaf Rudbeck, was in charge of anatomy, botany, and zoology. He left all his teaching to his assistant, Nils Rosén. Unfortunately, Rosén was in Holland earning his degree.

When Linnaeus first arrived in Uppsala, he could not find a job. He soon ran out of money. In his autobiography, he wrote that "he had to borrow to buy food and could not even pay to have his shoes soled, being obliged to lay paper in them. . . . He would gladly have returned to Stobaeus who had treated him so kindly, but he could not afford the journey. Besides, Dr. Stobaeus would have been extremely angry to meet again the youth for whom he had taken such an interest and who had deserted him without even asking his advice."[1]

New Friends

The following spring, Linnaeus met Peter Artedi. The two young men were very different in looks and personality. Artedi was tall and solemn. Linnaeus was short, sturdy, and cheerful. But they both loved natural history. They wanted to study the entire plant and animal kingdoms. This was such a big undertaking that they decided to divide the work between them. Artedi took the amphibians, reptiles, and fish. Linnaeus took the birds and insects. Artedi was already working on classifying the parsley family, so Linnaeus said he would

After leaving Lund University, Linnaeus arrived at Uppsala University in 1728. This is the Medical Building at Uppsala.

organize the rest of the plant kingdom. They agreed on one more point. If one of them should die, the other would make sure that any unfinished work was published.

The other friend Linnaeus made that year was an elderly man he met in the university's botanical garden. The man asked Linnaeus the names of some plants and was impressed by his answers. He was even more impressed when he learned that Linnaeus had a collection of more than six hundred kinds of wildflowers. He invited Linnaeus to his home. Linnaeus then discovered that he had been talking to Dr. Olaf Celsius, one of the most important men in Uppsala. He was a professor of theology and dean of the cathedral.

Dr. Celsius took a liking to young Linnaeus. He not only granted him the use of his library, but he offered him a place to stay. Linnaeus was glad to accept. This would solve his money problem. To repay the doctor's kindness, Linnaeus helped him with a book he was writing on all the plants named in the Bible.

At that time, students often wrote New Year's poems to honor their favorite professor. Linnaeus was not much of a poet. Instead, he gave Dr. Celsius a scientific paper he had just written. It was about pollination in plants and explained the role of the stamen and pistil in the formation of seeds.

The Professor's Assistant

Celsius was delighted with Linnaeus's paper. He showed it to Professor Rudbeck, who was very interested. Soon after, Linnaeus applied to Rudbeck for a position as gardener at the university's botanical garden. He was disappointed when he did not get the job. Rudbeck, however, had something better in mind. He asked Linnaeus to teach botany.

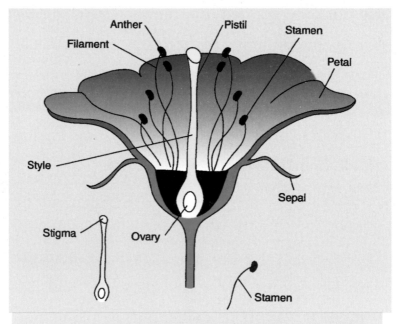

The parts of a flower. Linnaeus classified plants by the number and positions of the stamens in their flowers.

Although Linnaeus was only a second-year student, his lectures drew large crowds. Three or four hundred people showed up instead of the usual seventy or eighty students.

Rudbeck was pleased with his new assistant's success. He invited Linnaeus to move into his home and tutor his three youngest sons. The boys were part of a very large family. Rudbeck had been married three times and had twenty-four children!

Although he now had two jobs (teaching and tutoring), Linnaeus found time for his own work. The fact that so many plants did not fit into the existing methods of classification troubled him. He began to develop a new system. He grouped flowers into twenty-four classes based on the number and position of their stamens. He divided the classes into orders based on the pistils. The orders were divided into genera (the plural of *genus*) by the form of the fruit. Linnaeus was only twenty-three, but he had taken a giant step toward reorganizing the classification of the entire plant kingdom.

Linnaeus lived in Professor Rudbeck's house while tutoring the professors youngest sons. He later lived here with his own family.

During the long winter evenings, Rudbeck often told Linnaeus stories of his youthful adventures. As a young man, he had traveled north to Lapland, where he made drawings and notes of the many unusual things he saw. He collected flowers and brought back animal skins and bones. Unfortunately, all his work was lost in a terrible fire that raged through Uppsala in 1702. He encouraged Linnaeus to undertake a similar journey. Linnaeus was eager to go, but the trip would be expensive.

In March 1731, Rudbeck's assistant, Nils Rosén, returned from Holland with a degree in medicine. He quickly became the most popular doctor in Uppsala. He took over the teaching of anatomy at the university. He also wanted to teach botany, but Rudbeck decided that Linnaeus was the better botanist. Rosén was annoyed. His attitude upset Linnaeus, who did not like to be "the object of jealousy."[2]

Several months later, Linnaeus and Rudbeck's wife had a disagreement. She no longer wanted him to tutor the children. Dr. Rudbeck was not brought into the quarrel, but Linnaeus was forced to find somewhere else to live. To add to his worries, he learned that his mother was seriously ill.

Linnaeus went home to Stenbrohult for Christmas. Before going, he had applied to the Royal Society of Sciences at Uppsala for a grant to go plant hunting in Lapland. He hoped they would give him the money. Then he would have a good reason to stay away from Uppsala for a while.

Lapland Adventure

CHRISTINA LINNAEA WAS NOT ENTHUSIASTIC WHEN her son told her about his travel plans. Lapland was a wild and rugged area that covered the northern parts of Norway, Sweden, and Finland. The Lapps did not live in just one country. They followed the migration of the reindeer herds, traveling up into the high mountains in the summer and back down to the forests in the winter.

Carl Linnaeus explained that as well as collecting new plants and animals, he would be looking for valuable minerals. Also, he was curious about the customs of the native people of Lapland. These reasons were not enough for Christina. She hoped that the Royal Society would decide not to fund the trip.

Nils Linnaeus was more supportive. He told Carl that if he thought that the journey would advance his career, then he should ask for God's guidance and help. As it turned out, the journey did make a big difference to Carl's future.

From Umeå to Lycksele

In April, Linnaeus heard that the Royal Society had awarded him a grant. It was less than he had asked for, but he did not think twice about accepting. He spent the next month getting ready for his expedition. Lightweight gear makes a trip into the wilderness much easier now than it was in those days. In his leather bag, Linnaeus packed an extra shirt, nightcaps, a comb, an inkhorn (a small bottle to hold ink), a pen case, and a magnifying glass. He took along a gauze veil to protect against insects, his journal, manuscripts on birds and plants, and lots of sheets of paper for pressing plants.

Linnaeus set off on May 22, 1732, the day before his twenty-fifth birthday. He wore "trousers quite elegant in leather" and "a

In the spring of 1732, Linnaeus journeyed north to study the plants and animals of Lapland. Linnaeus is pictured here in Lappish native dress.

braided wig."[1] His sword hung at his side. As he headed north, everything he saw delighted him. He often got down from his horse to pick a flower or to examine a rock. It took him eleven days to reach the first goal, the northern city of Umeå.

From Umeå, Linnaeus headed west toward Lycksele. It was raining hard. His horse walked carefully along the narrow stony path. Toward evening, he came upon a group of women who were shredding aspen bark to feed to their cows and goats. When he asked if they could provide him with supper, they offered him a small game bird called a woodcock. It had been shot, dried, and salted the previous year. To his surprise, it was quite tasty. That night he slept between reindeer skins and laid his head on a pillow stuffed with reindeer hair.

The next day, he was on the trail early. In spite of bad roads and miserable weather, Linnaeus did not miss even the smallest plants. He recorded everything in his journal. He was especially interested in mosses and lichens.

One of the things that interested Linnaeus the most during his trip to Lapland was lichens. Lichens form the main part of a reindeer's diet.

Lichens, which form the main part of the reindeer diet, grow in great abundance in the north.

When the roads became impassable, Linnaeus hired a guide and continued the journey by boat. On reaching Lycksele, he called on the local pastor and his wife. They invited him to stay for a few days so that they could let the Lapps know that he was coming. The Lapps did not always welcome strangers. The next day, however, was warm. The river was rising due to melting snow. If he delayed, travel would not be possible.

Linnaeus and his guide were on the river all day. They continued their journey through the night. Because they were so far north, the sun disappeared below the horizon for only about an hour and a half. Later Linnaeus wrote that he had been "led into a new world, and when I came up into it, I didn't know if I was in Asia or Africa, for the soil, the landscape, and all the plants were unknown to me."[2]

The few people Linnaeus and his guide met were too busy fishing to stop and give them food. The guide went on ahead in search of help. When he came back, Linnaeus could not tell if the wild-looking creature who was with him was a man or a woman. This "Fury," as he called her in his journal, turned out to be a woman with a great tangle of black hair. Linnaeus asked her for food, and she offered him several fish. This is how Linnaeus described the scene:

> I looked at the raw fish, whose mouths were full of worms, and the sight took away my appetite. . . . I asked if I could get reindeer tongues, which the Lapps dry and sell . . . but she said it was not possible. "Then reindeer cheese?" "Yes, but it is nearly six miles away." "If you have any, could I buy one or two?" She replied, "I would not want you to die of hunger in my country."[3]

The Far North

After buying a small cheese, Linnaeus retraced his steps to Lycksele. He then returned to Umeå. He was soon ready to be on his way again, this time heading north. His journal entry for June 15, 1732, provides a picture of some of the discomforts and dangers of this stage of the journey. A cloud of gnats "seemed to occupy the whole atmosphere, especially when I traveled through damp meadows. They filled my mouth, nose and eyes. Luckily they did not bite or sting, though they almost choked me.

"Just at sunset I reached the town of Old

Linnaeus's travels took him to Lapland in the north of Sweden.

Piteå. Near the landing spot stood a gibbet with a couple of wheels on which lay the bodies of two Finlanders without heads. These men had been executed for highway robbery and murder."[4]

Soon after this, Linnaeus came upon some pearl fishermen. They were pulling mussels out of the river with long tongs. To find one pearl, they had to open several thousand mussels. This chance meeting turned out to be important to Linnaeus later. He figured that the pearl was caused by something being wrong inside the mussel. Thinking about this, he wrote, "Anyone who could induce this illness in mussels could make them produce pearls; if one could, what could be more profitable?"[5]

The route then took Linnaeus up into the Lapland Alps, where he shared a crowded hut with sixteen Lapps. He told them he wanted to travel to the coast of Norway. A seventy-year-old man and his friend, who was about fifty, offered to show him the way. By the time the three of them reached the coast, young Linnaeus was exhausted. The Lapps were still full of energy, although they had carried all the gear. Linnaeus wondered what kept them so healthy. He decided that the pure air and water must be partly responsible. The Lapp outlook and lifestyle also promoted good health. They were not jealous people. They rarely quarreled. They were moderate in their eating and drinking. Later in his career, Linnaeus gave lectures on health and diet. His ideas were ahead of his time, and many are accepted to this day.

Back in Uppsala

5

WHEN LINNAEUS UNPACKED THE SPECIMENS FROM his Lapland journey, his room began to look like a museum. Lapp clothing was displayed on one wall, and a bookcase took up another. He had thousands of kinds of insects, as well as boxes and boxes of shells and stones. Pots of rare plants covered the tables. His herbarium included more than three thousand species of pressed flowers. In one corner of the room, thirty different kinds of tame birds perched on the branches of a tree!

Linnaeus and Nils Rosén were still at odds with one another. Linnaeus was too busy teaching botany and writing a book on the flowers of Lapland to attend Rosén's anatomy classes. This annoyed Rosén. The fact that

After his return from Lapland, Carl Linnaeus began work on his book *Flora Lapponica*. When translated into English, the title is *Flowers of Lapland*.

Linnaeus's botany lectures were more popular than ever did not help matters.

When Linnaeus went home to Stenbrohult for Christmas, he enjoyed telling his family about his Lapland adventure. But he was worried about his mother's health. When he returned to Uppsala, he was afraid that he would not see her again. His fears turned out to be true. Christina Linnaea died the next summer, in 1733.

Visiting Falun

The following Christmas, Linnaeus did not go home. Instead he accepted an invitation from Claes Sohlberg, a fellow student, to visit his family. The Sohlbergs lived in Falun, in the central Swedish province of Dalarna. After working such long hours in Uppsala, Linnaeus threw himself into Falun's social life.

Claes Sohlberg's father was an inspector of the mines. He asked Linnaeus if he would like to go down a copper mine. This turned out to be the high point—or the low point—of his stay in Falun. Linnaeus compared it to visiting hell. After climbing down swaying ladders, he crawled through places so narrow that he had to turn sideways to get through. The miners carried torches in their mouths. Linnaeus wrote, "There is a constant risk of sudden death from the collapse of a roof, so that they can never feel safe for a single second. The great depth, the

Students at Uppsala University watched dissections in the anatomy theater. Although Linnaeus was a medical student, he was too busy teaching classes to attend anatomy lectures.

dark and the danger, made my hair stand on end with fright, and I wished for one thing only—to be back again on the surface."[1]

Linnaeus returned to Uppsala with more boxes of rocks and minerals. He was happy to have another collection to arrange. He started to write a book on a system for classifying minerals.

By now, Linnaeus had been a student for seven years. His goal was to be a professor of botany. For that, though, he needed a degree in medicine from a foreign university. Holland was a gathering place for the scholars of Europe and also an important center of printing. Linnaeus hoped that he could have his manuscripts published there. He tried to think of some way to pay for the journey.

Another Excursion

The arrival of a letter from the governor of Dalarna, whom Linnaeus had met at a party in Falun, saved him from having to deal with the financial problem right then. The governor wanted Linnaeus to make a complete study of the natural history of Dalarna. Linnaeus was delighted with the idea.

This time Linnaeus did not travel alone. He was now a well-known explorer. Lots of students were eager to go along, paying their own way. Linnaeus settled on seven young men, including his friend Claes. Each student had a different job. One looked after the horses. Another arranged for places to stay along the route. Sometimes they slept in barns; sometimes they boarded with the village pastor. Other students recorded the samples of plants, animals, and minerals. Someone took notes on the way of life of the people they met on their travels.

The governor was so pleased with the expedition's report that he invited Linnaeus to stay on at Falun and teach his sons. The job left Linnaeus plenty of time for his own writing and studying.

Later in the year, Claes Sohlberg's father offered to pay Linnaeus to travel to Holland with his son. Linnaeus was to help Claes with his studies. Linnaeus quickly accepted. He could finally complete his degree. He was also eager to visit the famous Botanical Gardens in Amsterdam, where many of the plants had come from the New World.

It was now Christmas again. Linnaeus took another well-earned break from his work. At a party, he met a young woman named Sara Lisa Moraea. She was eighteen years old. Linnaeus was twenty-seven. They promptly fell in love.

Sara Lisa's father was the leading doctor in Falun. He did not like the idea of his daughter marrying a poor botanist. Sara Lisa begged, and her father finally gave in. He agreed that she and Carl could become engaged if they waited for three years before they married. Linnaeus was to go to Holland with Claes Sohlberg as planned. Dr. Moraeus probably thought that a lot could happen in three years.

6

Clifford's Garden

WHEN LINNAEUS AND SOHLBERG ARRIVED IN
Holland, Linnaeus wasted no time in getting his
medical degree. He handed in a thesis that he
had written in Sweden on the cause of malaria.
Although Linnaeus did not know that malaria
was passed to people by mosquitoes, he was on
the right track. He had noticed that the sickness
was common near clay soil deposits. Clay, used
to make building bricks, was dug from pits
next to where people lived. Water collected in
these pits and provided a breeding place for
mosquitoes.

The next step toward the medical degree was
an oral exam. Linnaeus was required to diagnose
a case of jaundice. Finally, he defended his thesis
in a public debate. He earned his degree in less

than two weeks! Of course, he had already spent seven years as a university student in Sweden.

In the end, Sohlberg's father did not give Linnaeus the money he had promised. The two young men drifted apart. Now that he had completed his medical degree, Linnaeus could have returned to Sara Lisa Moraea in Sweden. But first, he wanted to meet some of the leading scientists in Holland.

Systema Naturae

One of the first Dutch scientists that Linnaeus got to know was Dr. Johan Gronovius, an important botanist. Linnaeus showed him a manuscript describing his new system for classifying plants. Gronovius was so impressed that he offered to help pay for the cost of having it printed. *Systema Naturae* (A System of Nature) was published in 1735.

In *Systema Naturae*, Linnaeus gave botanists a set of working rules for classifying plants.

He divided nature into three kingdoms, using these characteristics: "Stones grow; plants grow and live; animals grow, live, and feel."[1] The plant kingdom was divided into twenty-four classes, according to the number and position of the stamens. The classes were divided into orders, and the orders into genera.

Although Linnaeus's system greatly advanced the study of botany, it is no longer used. Some plants that are not closely related ended up in the same group. Linnaeus lived a hundred years before Charles Darwin wrote *The Origin of Species*. Darwin's theory of evolution explained how species can change over time. This gave botanists a clearer understanding of plant relationships. They could then develop a more logical system of classification.

The first edition of *Systema Naturae* was a short book. However, a lot of information was packed into its fourteen large pages. Linnaeus revised *Systema Naturae* many times during the next thirty years. In later editions, he adopted the binomial system of nomenclature. The twelfth edition, completed in 1768, ran to three volumes and 2,300 pages.

Traded for a Book

To stay in Holland longer, Linnaeus needed to find a way to support himself. His problem was solved when Dr. Johannes Burman invited him to be his guest. In return, he was to help Burman with a book he was writing. Shortly after, Linnaeus met a rich businessman, George Clifford, who was a director of the Dutch East India Company. He was a keen botanist and zoologist. The trading ships brought him many unusual plants and animals from abroad. His country estate was known throughout Holland for its botanical garden and private zoo.

George Clifford was amazed by the way Linnaeus could classify plants that he had never seen before simply by opening up the flower and studying the stamens and pistils. Linnaeus was equally amazed by Clifford's wonderful garden. The hothouses were overflowing with tropical plants from India and other faraway places.

Linnaeus could think of nothing he wanted more than to spend all his time studying and describing the flowers in Clifford's garden.

These are Brugmansia, more commonly known as angels' trumpets. Clifford's greenhouses were filled with such beautiful and exotic tropical plants.

Clifford, who was often sick, liked the idea of having a live-in doctor. He asked Linnaeus to join his household. However, Burman did not want to lose Linnaeus's help. The problem was solved when Burman admired a book in Clifford's library. "I happen to have two copies," Clifford said. "I will give you one if you will let me have Linnaeus."[2] So Carl Linnaeus was traded for a rare book!

Linnaeus was as gifted at raising plants as he was at naming them. A banana tree that grew in one of Clifford's hothouses had never bloomed. Linnaeus repotted the plant in rich soil. He let the soil dry out and then soaked it, copying the pattern of tropical rainstorms. To everyone's delight, the plant not only bloomed, but also produced fruit. Botanists from all over Holland came to see the miracle plant.

Early that summer, Linnaeus had run into Peter Artedi, his old friend from Uppsala. They were both so busy that they did not meet again until September. Artedi was writing a book on the classification of fishes. The two young men spent a long time looking over Artedi's notes and discussing his ideas. It turned out to be the last time they met. A few days later, Artedi fell into a canal and drowned.

Linnaeus was terribly upset when he heard the tragic news. He remembered the pact that they had made back in Uppsala. If one of them should die, the other would make sure his unfinished work was published. Linnaeus completed Artedi's book from his notes. It came out in 1738. Later, he named a plant in the parsley family *Artedia* in his friend's honor.

Further Travels

In the summer of 1736, Linnaeus visited England. He did not speak English. In fact, he had not learned the language of any country he had visited. He could speak with educated people in Latin. Linnaeus made friends easily, but there were botanists in England who did not want to like him. He had turned the naming system of plants upside down. He had thrown out old names, replacing them with new ones to fit into his system. However, when they met him, they were won over. They soon agreed that he had an amazing grasp of botany. It was almost impossible to show him a plant that he could not name.

When he returned to Holland, Linnaeus threw himself into writing *Hortus Cliffortianus*, a book about the rare plants in Clifford's greenhouses. The description for each plant had to fit only that species. This was exacting work. It required research and detailed observations. Although Linnaeus worked long hours then, he looked back on this period in Holland as the best time of his life. He was doing the work he loved, and Clifford treated him like a son.

In the fall of 1737, overwork caught up with Linnaeus. He became ill and wanted to return to Sweden. But everyone begged him not to go yet. He agreed to stay on through the winter.

In early spring, Linnaeus received disturbing news from Falun. One of his friends was courting Sara Lisa! It had not been hard for the friend to persuade Sara Lisa that Carl's true love was

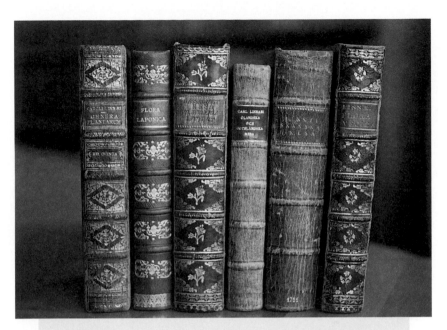

Linnaeus returned from Holland with a medical degree and a solid start on the many books that would make him famous.

botany. Linnaeus had earned his degree in two weeks, but he had been gone for three years. Sara Lisa had reason to be tired of waiting.

Linnaeus began to make plans to return to Sweden, but he fell ill again. It was May before he was well enough to travel. In spite of the time he had lost, he still did not go straight home. He made a side trip to France, spending a month meeting scientists in Paris.

Linnaeus's first stop in Sweden was Stenbrohult. Nils Linnaeus was proud to see copies of all the books that his son had published in the three years he had been gone. After spending two weeks with his father, Linnaeus set off for Falun. There he found Sara Lisa waiting for him.

The New Doctor

DR. MORAEUS STILL HAD DOUBTS ABOUT HIS FUTURE son-in-law. He thought that Linnaeus needed a steady job with a good income before he married Sara Lisa. Moraeus had no idea how greatly respected the young botanist was by foreign scientists. Linnaeus found it hard to come home and find that no one in Sweden cared "how many sleepless nights and weary hours"[1] he had spent on bringing order to the plant kingdom.

When Linnaeus set off for Stockholm to start a medical practice, he left Sara Lisa behind in Falun. At first, he was discouraged with his prospects. He put up a sign, but no one came. He complained that "there was nobody who would put even a servant under my care."[2] Once again, he was worried about money, but his luck soon turned. One of his first patients was the wife of a senator. Linnaeus gave her a new kind of medicine that he had learned about in his recent visit to France. The medicine worked. The senator's wife told Queen Ulrika about Dr. Linnaeus. The queen came to see him, too. From then on, the new doctor had all the patients he could handle.

Linnaeus soon became acquainted with most of the important people in Stockholm. One of them was Count Carl Tessin, a man who was very interested in science. He arranged for Linnaeus to give lectures on plants. He suggested Linnaeus for the position of doctor to the Navy. Later, Linnaeus became the first president of the Royal Swedish Academy of Sciences in Stockholm.

Wedding Bells

Once again, Linnaeus was working very hard. Today he would be called a workaholic. Within a year, he proved that he could support a wife in style. He and Sara Lisa Moraea were married

Carl Linnaeus was able to prove to Dr. Moraeus that he would be able to support Moraeus's daughter, Sara Lisa. Linnaeus's wedding portrait is shown here.

in Falun in June 1739. After a month's vacation, Linnaeus returned to his busy life in Stockholm. Sara Lisa stayed behind with her parents. Carl and Sara Lisa paid a price for their long separations. They did not have a happy marriage.

Linnaeus planted a botanical garden in Stockholm, where he grew plants that were useful in medicine. He led field trips to parks and out into the countryside. Although he was doing well as a doctor, in his heart Linnaeus was a botanist. His ambition was still to be a professor of botany in Uppsala. He nearly got his wish in March 1740, when Olaf Rudbeck died. However, his old rival, Nils Rosén, was offered the job. Linnaeus was furious. He scoffed at the university's choice, saying that Rosén "can't even recognize a nettle when he sees one."[3]

In January 1741, Sara Lisa Linnaea gave birth to a son. The baby was named Carl after his father. Sara Lisa was still staying with her parents in Falun. Linnaeus wrote to his wife

In January of 1741, Sara Lisa gave birth to a son while in Falun, Sweden. Carl Linnaeus was busy at work in Stockholm at the time.

telling her that he was overjoyed. He did not, however, rush home to see his family.

Öland and Gotland

Soon after baby Carl's birth, the other professor of medicine at Uppsala retired. Linnaeus applied for his job. While he was waiting to hear about it, he was given the chance to go off on another adventure. The government asked Linnaeus to lead an expedition to the islands of Öland and Gotland. He was to look for minerals and to collect plants that could be used for medicines and for dye. He was also to look for clay soil that could be used to make fine pottery. Sweden was a poor country. Finding more natural resources would help the economy. This was exactly the sort of challenge that Linnaeus loved.

In May, Linnaeus learned that the job at Uppsala was his. He set off on the expedition, feeling very lucky. On his way through Växjö, he stopped in to see his old teacher, Dr. Rothman. The doctor was proud that the student that no

This lovely pink flower is an orchid. Linnaeus was pleasantly surprised to see orchids blooming in Öland.

one else had believed in was now a famous scientist.

On reaching Öland, Linnaeus was thrilled by the sight of wild orchids. He had seen them in France, but had not expected to find them in Sweden. Today, people still travel to Öland to admire the orchids in the spring.

Linnaeus tramped all over the island of Öland, looking at everything. He was fascinated by rune stones from the Viking age. He found other reminders of the past. He was greatly impressed by the ancient ruins of Ismanstorpsborg. We still do not know who built the massive walls there. Linnaeus wrote, "In comparison to the other ruins . . . this was like a capital among hamlets. . . . There were rooms in all directions, but the plan could not be clearly discerned, since the ruin was so overgrown with bushes and trees."[4]

Linnaeus kept telling his helpers on the expedition to keep their eyes open. It was important to notice everything. When some of the local people overheard him, they grew

In May of 1741, Linnaeus went to explore the wildlife on Öland, an island off the coast of Sweden. Linnaeus was excited to find rune stones that date back to the days of the Vikings.

suspicious. At this time, Sweden was on the verge of war with Russia. The islanders thought Linnaeus and his helpers could be Russian spies! Linnaeus had to add a local man to his team to explain that they were only interested in the plants and rocks.

Linnaeus's *Öland and Gotland Journey* was published in 1741. It was the first book in which he used binomial nomenclature throughout. It was also his first book written in Swedish and not in Latin. He defended this choice, saying that if people were allowed to write only in Latin, "the world would know less today than in fact it does."[5] But Linnaeus had worried that a scientific book written in Swedish would not be read. He need not have worried. The book, whose language is colorful and easy to understand, is still popular. Linnaeus's example and his works no doubt influence the Swedish people's love of nature today.

The Professor

WHEN LINNAEUS ARRIVED IN UPPSALA IN OCTOBER 1741, he was a happy man. He was now a professor. He was at last living under the same roof as Sara Lisa and baby Carl. The only thing that kept life from being perfect was that he had to teach anatomy and the other medical sciences. Nils Rosén taught all branches of natural history, including botany. As it turned out, this problem was easily solved. The two men switched jobs.

The Linnaeus family moved into Olaf Rudbeck's old stone house. It was where Linnaeus had lived as a student ten years earlier. The house stood on the grounds of the university botanical gardens. The gardens had been badly neglected. Linnaeus wrote to friends in Holland and England asking for rare plants. He built new greenhouses and a tropical hothouse. Seven years later, the plant list ran to three thousand species.

Linnaeus collected unusual animals as well as plants. He was particularly fond of monkeys and parrots. One of his monkeys was a gift from Queen Ulrika. It had been a troublemaker in the palace, where it liked to steal silver buckles from the courtiers' shoes. Linnaeus's favorite parrot perched on his shoulder at mealtimes. If he was late coming to lunch, the parrot would repeat "Twelve o'clock, Mr. Carl!" until he appeared. The parrot also called "Come in!" when hearing a knock at the door. Sometimes a visitor would then walk into the room and be puzzled to find no one there![1]

Lectures and Outings

Linnaeus was a very popular teacher. He always lectured to overflow crowds. Students were attracted by his enthusiasm and the range of his subject matter. He often lectured on nutrition

After his return to Uppsala, Linnaeus restored the university's botanical gardens, which had been neglected.

and even on parenting. He said that children should eat often, but should only eat a little at a time. He disagreed with the custom of tightly wrapping infants. He believed babies should not be christened during cold weather or with cold water. He said that brown cows give the best milk. Not all of his ideas were good science. Some were based on the superstitions of his time.

On Saturdays, Linnaeus led large groups of

students out into the countryside. Sometimes as many as a hundred and fifty people showed up. They all dressed alike in light, comfortable linen clothes. They carried butterfly nets and plant presses. These outings were similar to Linnaeus's earlier expeditions, but on a much bigger scale and closer to home. He chose someone to take notes and someone to look after discipline. Someone was chosen to shoot birds. In those days, bird-watchers carried guns instead of binoculars. When a rare specimen was found, a student sounded a bugle. Everyone gathered around Linnaeus to learn about the specimen. At lunchtime, a table was set up with twenty places. The students who had made the most exciting finds won a spot at the table with Linnaeus.

At the end of the day, they marched back into town, waving banners, sounding horns, and beating drums. Linnaeus was in the lead. When they reached the botanical gardens, a cheer went up: "Long live science! Long live Linnaeus!"

Linnaeus was an enthusiastic and well-liked teacher. His students enjoyed helping him with his work. This scene depicts Linnaeus (in the lower right, sitting between two men) classifying plants in his garden with the help of three pupils.

As you might guess, some of the less popular professors complained about the noise!

Family Matters

Meantime, the Linnaeus family was growing. In 1743, when little Carl was two, Lisa Stina was born. Another baby girl was born the following year, but she did not live long. Then came

Louisa in 1749 and Sara Stina in 1751. Another son, Johannes, was born in 1754 and died in 1757. Before the days of modern medicines, many children died young. The Linnaeus's last child was born in 1757. Little Sophia would not have lived without her father's skill as a doctor.

He described the birth in a letter to a friend: "Last Tuesday evening my wife bore me a daughter. She had a very difficult delivery and the girl was stillborn or died at birth, but nevertheless we blew air into her. . . . After a quarter of an hour she began to breath a little. . . . Now she seems fairly well; but my wife is very weak, God help her!"[2]

Sophia thrived and grew up to be Linnaeus's favorite child. However, in spite of his lectures on parenting, he was not always a good father, and his was not always a happy household. Young Carl was taught at home. Linnaeus was determined that his son would follow in his footsteps, so Carl learned a lot about botany. Most other subjects were neglected. Linnaeus did not seem to remember that he had chosen not to be a clergyman like his father. Young Carl feared his parents more than he loved them.

The girls, on the other hand, had no education at all. This was common at the time. And Linnaeus actively opposed any education for girls. His daughters were not allowed to have French lessons. He wanted them to grow up to be "hearty, strong

Sophia was the youngest and favorite of Linnaeus's children. In later years, she assisted her father in his work.

housekeepers, not fashionable dolls."[3] Once, when Linnaeus was away, Sara Lisa Linnaea enrolled Sophia in school. When Linnaeus returned, he soon put a stop to that idea.

During this period, Linnaeus published some of his most important work. Botanists agreed to accept the binomial names in *Species Plantarum*

(1753) as the correct names, and to stop using names given before that time. The tenth edition of *Systema Naturae* (1758) became the starting point for binomial names for animals. Linnaeus was the first scientist to recognize that whales are mammals. In the tenth edition, he no longer used the name Quadrupedia ("four legs") for higher animals. Instead he called them Mammalia.

Hammarby

In 1758, Linnaeus bought Hammarby, a summer home about six miles from Uppsala. As soon as the weather warmed up in the spring, the whole family moved out there. They stayed until fall. They all loved Hammarby. Linnaeus built a separate stone structure on a rocky hill behind the house to keep his precious collections safe from fire. He called this storeroom his museum.

Linnaeus used to attend the local church on Sunday mornings. His dog Pompe always accompanied him. Linnaeus did not like to sit

On Saturdays it was not unusual to find Linnaeus leading students on expeditions to look for rare forms of wildlife. Linnaeus kept his collection of plants at this museum in Hammarby.

through long services. After one hour, he would get up and walk out. When Linnaeus was sick, the little dog went to church by himself. Like his master, he always padded out at the end of an hour!

Linnaeus's students followed him to Hammarby. One of these students, Johan Fabricius, kept a journal. He painted a happy picture of summers spent with the Linnaeus family. On Sundays, everyone gathered at a farmhouse where the students stayed. They danced in the barn to the music of a violin. Sometimes Linnaeus watched from the sidelines. Other times he joined in, dancing with as much energy as his students. He liked to see young people enjoying themselves—the rowdier the better. Fabricius wrote, "I never shall forget those days, those hours, and it makes me happy whenever I recall them."[4]

The Apostles

AFTER LINNAEUS BECAME A PROFESSOR AT UPPSALA, he never lived outside Sweden again. His influence, however, reached far beyond Sweden's shores. Many of his students went overseas to look for plants in distant lands. The Linnaean system of naming allowed new plants to be fitted into the framework of known plants. This spurred scientists to find new specimens.

The students who went off on these scientific expeditions became known as Linnaeus's "apostles." This is a good name for them. An apostle is a kind of missionary. Linnaeus's students spread their teacher's fame throughout the world.

Looking for plants in foreign lands was dangerous work. Five of Linnaeus's students did not return. Forty-three-year-old Christopher Tärnström was the first apostle. He was a pastor with a wife and children. In 1746, he set off for China on an East India Company trading ship. Linnaeus hoped Tärnström would bring back a tea plant, or at least some seeds. Linnaeus also wanted some live goldfish. But Tärnström never reached China. He died of a tropical fever off the coast of Cambodia, in Southeast Asia. His death was a terrible blow to Linnaeus.

Flower Power

Two years later, Peter Kalm left for North America. First he went to Delaware, the home of many Swedish settlers. He then spent two and half years exploring Pennsylvania, New York, New Jersey, and Canada. Linnaeus was disappointed at how few letters he received from Kalm. However, when the young explorer came home, he was soon forgiven. Linnaeus was sick at the time. On seeing all the pressed flowers and seeds that Kalm brought back, Linnaeus claimed that "through joy at the plants, he no longer felt his illness."[1] In *Species Plantarum,* Linnaeus described seven hundred North American species. Ninety of them had been brought back by Kalm.

After hearing Linnaeus lecture on the plants of Egypt and Palestine, Fredrick Hasselquist made up his mind to see the plants in their native setting. Linnaeus tried to talk him out of going. Hasselquist was not a strong man. Linnaeus's worst fears came true. The young student died in Turkey, "like a lamp whose oil is consumed."[2] He owed a huge amount of money at the time of his death. His collections and manuscripts could not be sent back to Sweden until the debt was cleared. Linnaeus appealed to the queen, who was very interested in natural history. She took care of the debt. Linnaeus was amazed when he finally read Hasselquist's papers. He wrote, "God Bless the peerless Queen for letting me see them! . . . So admirable a travel journal has never before appeared."[3]

Peter Osbeck sailed for China in 1750 and returned safely two years later. He gave his

Often Linnaeus's students would visit foreign lands to collect specimens and spread the name of their teacher. One of his students, Peter Osbeck, returned from China with this tea set decorated with Linnaeus's favorite flower, the twinflower.

whole collection to Linnaeus. He also brought his professor a china tea set, decorated with twinflowers—Linnaeus's favorite flower.

When the Spanish Ambassador asked Linnaeus who should study the plants in his country, Linnaeus suggested Peter Löfling. Since he did such a good job, Löfling was sent to South America to collect plants for "the Spanish Court, the King of France, the Queen of Sweden, and Linnaeus."[4] Linnaeus was happy to be included in such famous company.

Circling the Globe

Daniel Solander was another apostle and a favorite student. When the young man was offered a job at the British Museum in 1763, Linnaeus asked an English friend, John Ellis, to look out for him. Linnaeus continued to take an interest in Solander. In a letter to Ellis in 1767, he wrote, "Pray persuade Solander to write to his excellent mother, who has not received a letter from her beloved son for several years."[5]

Solander sailed around the world with Captain Cook in 1768–1771. This was the beginning of a tradition of including young naturalists on voyages of exploration. Sixty-three years later, Charles Darwin, the most famous naturalist-explorer, sailed around the world in the *Beagle*. Darwin was only twenty-two when he started out on his five-year voyage. His theory of evolution was based on observations made on the voyage.

Carl Thunberg was also widely traveled. After spending three years in South Africa, he visited Japan in 1775. At that time, foreigners were not welcome there. Thunberg collected plants in secret. He was so eager to learn more about Japanese plants that he went through the pig and cattle food every day looking for specimens to add to his herbarium. When he got to know some Japanese doctors, he taught them Linnaeus's system of classification. Like the other apostles, he was not afraid to put his life on the line while spreading the fame of his beloved teacher.

10

Prince of Botanists

LINNAEUS'S FATHER DIED IN MAY 1748. HIS LAST words were about his son. "Carl is not here," he said. "Carl has brought me much happiness."[1] Linnaeus was saddened by Nils's death. To make matters worse, his career was not going smoothly, although most of the problems were minor. The university was enforcing new rules. Professors needed permission to travel more than seven miles from Uppsala. Anyone who missed the beginning of the academic year would lose pay. The most annoying rule was that professors would be fined for publishing books in another country. At another time, Linnaeus would have taken this in his stride, but he felt that the publishing rule was directed at him. He was the only professor to whom it applied. When a friend complained about the way his botany students dressed and behaved on field trips, Linnaeus hardly slept for two months. He could understand some of the older and less successful professors' being jealous, but this was a trusted friend.

During this period, Linnaeus suffered periods of depression. But for long stretches, he enjoyed life as much as before. He still worked as hard as ever. Between 1749 and 1769, he wrote a hundred and seventy papers on everything from three-toed woodpeckers to the cause of epilepsy. His papers filled ten volumes. He also wrote several other books. In addition, he was busy with lectures, his students, and his family. He also found time to write letters to his many friends in Sweden and abroad.

The Pearl Business

Buying his country place at Hammarby had once again left Linnaeus short of money. He recalled the pearl fishermen he had watched in Lapland. Would it be possible to make artificial

As he grew older, Carl Linnaeus was awarded many honors. He was even knighted by the King of Sweden, which made him a nobleman.

pearls? He had an idea of how it could be done and decided to try it. He attached a tiny piece of limestone to a silver wire. Then he bored a hole in the shell of a mussel he had collected from the Fyris River. He inserted the limestone through the hole and fastened the wire to the shell. He put the mussel back in the river. Six years later, the rough limestone was completely covered. The mussel had made a large pearl.

At first, there was little interest in Linnaeus's experiment. Then, in 1761, Linnaeus was asked to bring his pearls to Stockholm. The government paid him two thousand dollars for his idea. In addition, he could choose his son or any other qualified person to be the next professor of botany at Uppsala.

Linnaeus was very happy. He could clear his debt and he could take care of young Carl's future. That same year, he was made a nobleman and became known as Carl von Linné. This is the name by which he is known in Sweden today, though he is still Carl Linnaeus to the rest of the world.

The Final Years

Linnaeus's health began to fail in 1763. Carl Jr. took over as professor of botany. Although he was a good botanist, he had taken no examinations. He was not a popular teacher like his father. Linnaeus continued to lecture whenever he could.

In May 1764, Linnaeus had a serious fever. Dr. Rosén was called in. He treated and cured his old rival. The two men, who had always had so much in common, finally became friends. Two years later, when Rosén suffered a similar illness, Linnaeus looked after him.

In 1772, Linnaeus was still having health problems, but he could not bring himself to stop working. In a letter to a friend, he wrote,

> You are right in saying that I ought not to work so hard. Latterly I have overtaxed my brain, and now, on Monday next, I have to begin my lecture course. I tried for one term letting my son lecture; but I was like the old cart-horse whose legs grew stiff before it had been a month in the stall.[2]

Linnaeus even took on the post of rector, the

head of the university, for the third time. (He had served as rector in 1750 and in 1759.) The students respected him so much that during those six months, they caused him no trouble at all. In the past, they had been very wild. In his final address, given in Latin, Linnaeus spoke of the pleasure that came from studying natural history. The next morning, students called on him to thank him. They asked him to publish a Swedish translation of his speech.

After suffering a stroke, Linnaeus was forced to spend the majority of his time at home. Shown here is Linnaeus's country estate in Hammarby, Sweden.

After he suffered a stroke, Linnaeus had trouble with his memory. This was sad for someone whose memory for names had amazed the world. But there were still good days. He had many important visitors, including King Gustaf III. One day in August 1775, the king arrived at Linnaeus's door. When he came into the house, the royal escorts were left sitting outdoors on their horses in the heavy rain. The king asked Sara Lisa Linnaea if there was anything he could do for her. She asked him to let his escorts come inside, so that they could dry off and have something to eat. The king was surprised, but he agreed.

Carl Linnaeus died on January 10, 1778. He wanted to be buried in the church at Hammarby. That was not to be. He was buried in Uppsala Cathedral. His funeral made a great impression on the mourners. One of them described the scene in these words:

> It was a still and gloomy evening, the darkness relieved only by the torches and lanterns carried by the mourners, the

After his death on January 10, 1778, Carl Linnaeus was buried at Uppsala Cathedral.

silence broken only by the murmur of the large crowds lining the streets and heavy tolling of the great bell.[3]

Linnaeus's library and all his collections were left to his widow and his children. Sir Joseph Banks, an Englishman, wanted to buy them. Carl Jr. refused. Carl moved the library and collections from Hammarby to Uppsala and took over their care. The collections were suffering from the effects of moisture.

Carl died late in 1783, less than six years after his father. Sara Lisa Linnaea inherited the collections. She wrote to Banks, asking if he was still interested. Banks learned this while he was giving a breakfast party. He was no longer interested, but one of his guests was. James Edward Smith, a twenty-four-year-old medical student, bought Linnaeus's great collections and books for a thousand guineas. He got a bargain. The collections included 19,000 plants, 3,198 insects, 1,564 shells, about 3,000 letters, and 3,000 books.

The people of Sweden were furious when

they learned that Linnaeus's collections were leaving the country. However, these items have been well cared for. Smith founded the Linnaean Society of London. The collections are still at the society's headquarters in Burlington House. Scientists from all over the world travel there to see the famous manuscripts and original specimens. They treat the work of Carl Linnaeus, the Prince of Botanists, with admiration and respect.

11

Before and After Linnaeus

THE SCIENCE OF NAMING GOES BACK TO THE Ancient Greeks. Aristotle named and described more than five hundred species of animals. He divided them into those that were "bloodless" and those that were "blooded." The bloodless ones were what we now call invertebrates, animals without backbones. The blooded ones were vertebrates, animals with backbones.[1] Plants were grouped by their form of growth— trees, bushes, or herbs.

After a long period of neglect, the sixteenth century saw a renewed interest in science. Casper Bauhin, a Swiss doctor and botanist, described more than six thousand species of plants. He did not agree with giving plants long Latin names. Sometimes he managed to reduce the name to two words—a binomial. But he did not think of this as a universal system. Linnaeus later used many of the names that Bauhin had introduced. He named a genus of showy orchid trees *Bauhinia* in the Swiss botanist's honor.

John Ray was an important English botanist in the seventeenth century. He was the son of a village blacksmith. His mother was a healer and herbalist. At the age of sixteen, Ray entered Cambridge University, where he studied languages, mathematics, and natural history. In 1660, he published his *Catalogue of Cambridge Plants*. He went on to write books on other groups of plants and animals. Unlike Linnaeus, Ray used many features—flowers, seeds, fruits and roots—when classifying plants.

Joseph Tournefort was another botanist who laid the foundation for Linnaeus's work. In 1700–1702 he traveled from his native France to Greece and then to the Orient. He brought back more than a thousand new kinds of plants. He classified flowers by looking at features of the petals. Linnaeus used this method until he switched to looking at the number of stamens and pistils.

The Origin of Species

Linnaeus's method was simple to learn and to use. Binomial names were easy to remember. The timing was right for providing a practical way of classifying and naming plants and animals. Explorers were coming back from the New World with thousands of specimens that all needed names.

While Linnaeus was "spending sleepless nights and weary hours" naming plants, he thought that this was a task that had an end.[2] Some day, every plant and animal would have its own name.

One hundred years later, that belief was shattered by a book called *On the Origin of Species by Natural Selection*, by Charles Darwin. In it, he explained how new species could arise. Darwin was a quiet, shy man who did not set out to change the world. For years, he worried about how people would react to his ideas. Long before his book was finished, he told his friend Joseph Hooker that he was sure that species could change over time. He added that this was like "confessing a murder."[3]

Darwin's theory of evolution changed the job description for taxonomists. Before Darwin, their job was to identify and name new species. After Darwin, taxonomists still named new species. But they also studied relationships between species. They took evolution into account. They tried to arrange plants in a series from the most primitive to the most advanced. They looked at a wide range of characters.

Clades and DNA

In the 1930s, Willi Hennig came up with a new way of thinking about relationships. Hennig was a German entomologist, or insect specialist. His method of classification is known as cladistics. The name comes from the Greek word *clade*, which means branch. A clade is a group of organisms that share a common ancestor. Members of a clade are more closely related to one another than to organisms outside the clade.

Hennig's new taxonomy challenged some established ideas. For example, scientists thought that all green algae were related. It seemed obvious that they all belonged in the same group. But a study of cell division and other features showed that some green algae are more closely related to land plants than they are to other green algae. Cladistics also led to the discovery that dinosaurs and birds are more closely related to each other than they are to reptiles, such as lizards. At first, cladistics was not widely accepted. Taxonomists now see it as a useful way of studying relationships

We have amazing new technical tools that help us see features that were invisible in the past. With an electron microscope we can see each hair on a fly. Linnaeus described species by looking at the anthers inside a flower. Now we can see the complex patterns on a grain of pollen inside the anther. Each species has its own distinct pollen pattern.

Another way that plant scientists can tell species apart is by looking at the genetic code. They extract the plants' DNA, usually from a small piece of leaf. They can then use the DNA to identify and classify plants in much the same way that detectives use DNA to identify a criminal or victim of a crime.

Collecting and Collections

Although modern taxonomists use up-to-date technology, some things have not changed since Linnaeus's time. Entomologists still chase butterflies with nets. They collect moths that cluster around a light. They turn over stones in a stream, looking for mayflies. The specimens are often prepared in the same old-fashioned way. The body of a butterfly or moth is pierced with a pin. Its wings are then spread flat on a spreading board. Once the specimen is dry, it is labeled and transfered to a drawer in a museum. In some museums all the information about the specimen—its name, and where and when it was

This botanist is preserving her specimen using the same method of pressing and mounting that Linnaeus used.

Ribes sanguineum Pursh
var. sanguineum

Scott Sundberg   2002
Oregon State University

RIBES SANGUINEUM Pursh

USA, Oregon, Lane County: Crow Road,
15 miles

L.F. Henderson 14247   10 April 1932

HERBARIUM OF THE UNIVERSITY OF OREGON
EUGENE, OREGON, U.S.A.

HERBARIUM
111442
UNIVERSITY OF OREGON

An example of a preserved plant specimen.

found—are written on a label. In other museums, each specimen gets its own bar code.

Botanists preserve plants in the same way that Linnaeus did. The plant is laid between sheets of blotting paper and newspaper. Then it is squashed flat in a flower press. After it is completely dry, it is mounted on a sheet of paper, using glue. It is stored in a cabinet in a herbarium. Linnaeus would feel right at home in a modern herbarium.

More and Less

Linnaeus gave the potato and the tomato their names—*Solanum tuberosum* and *Solanum lycopersicum*. At that time, there were twenty-three species in the genus *Solanum*. In 1852, a French botanist listed nine hundred species in the genus. Now there are more than two thousand species in that one genus! Naming all the plants in the world has turned out to be a bigger job than Linnaeus could have imagined. New species of plants, insects, and bacteria are constantly being discovered.

Unfortunately, at the same time, the count is going down. Many species of plants and animals are becoming extinct. That means they are gone forever. Some of them were never given a name. One of the main reasons for extinction is loss of habitat. For example, rainforest destruction eliminates the only place where some plants and animals can live. Another cause of extinction is pollution of rivers and streams. Global climate change will have an even bigger effect on extinction of species.

The big challenges we face make the role of the taxonomist more important than ever before. We need to understand how species are related. We need to know how they interact with each other and how they depend on one another. We also need to have names for these species. It is hard to save something that has no name. Names are important. We need people like Carl Linnaeus who have a passion for naming.

Activities

Playing With Plants

According to Florence Caddy's biography of Carl Linnaeus, when he was a child, "[h]is toys were flowers."[1] Unfortunately, we do not know which games Carl played with flowers. Instead, here are two things to try with a potato:

1. To make a potato man, you need a potato and some grass seed. Cut a slice off the bottom of the potato so that it can stand. Now cut a slice off the top of the potato. Sprinkle grass seed on the cut surface. Keep the top of the potato moist.

   After a few days, the grass seeds will begin to sprout. Your potato man now has a head of green hair. You might want to add eyes, a nose, and a mouth to your potato man. When his hair grows long, you can give him a haircut.

2. Here is a magic trick to try on your friends: Challenge them to make the water level drop in a glass bowl by adding a potato.

   Cut both ends off the potato and scoop out some flesh to make a small cup on one end. Now stand the potato in the bowl of water. (You may have to shave off some potato to make it stand.) Put two teaspoonfuls of sugar in the hollow potato, adding a little water to make it dissolve.

   A few hours later, you will find that most of the water in the bowl has disappeared. The hollow potato has filled up with water. You have just shown how plants take in water. Water moves through cell walls going from the weak solution to a stronger solution. This process is called osmosis.

Flowers for the Fourth of July

With the help of a little food coloring, you can create a red, white, and blue bouquet from plain white flowers.

Materials:
- several fresh white flowers, such as carnations
- three small jars
- red and blue food coloring
- a little cooking oil

Procedure:
1. Fill the jars with water.
2. Add a few drops of red food coloring to one jar and blue food coloring to another.
3. Put some flowers in each jar.
4. Pour a little oil onto the water. This helps to keep the water from evaporating.

After two days, the flowers should have taken up some of the colored water in the jar. To make a two-colored flower, split the flower stem. Now put one part in the red solution and the other part in the blue solution.

Making a Flower Press

Linnaeus kept track of all the flowers he found by making an herbarium. It is not hard to dry flowers. You can glue a dried flower on a card to make stationery. You can laminate it between plastic and make a bookmark as a gift.

Materials:
- two sheets of Peg-Board about 8 x 12 inches (20 x 30 cm) or bigger
- two straps that are long enough to go around the boards (old belts would do)
- several sheets of blotting paper
- old newspapers
- fresh flowers

Procedure:
1. Place the flowers between two sheets of blotting paper.
2. Put the blotting paper sheets between pieces of newspaper.
3. Sandwich the newspaper package between pieces of Peg-Board.
4. Bind the Peg-Boards tightly with the straps.
5. Remove flowers after a few weeks.

You can also press flowers by placing them between sheets of blotting paper and piling heavy books on top. This method does not allow the flowers to dry thoroughly, and they may not keep as well.

Making an Indoor Garden

Linnaeus enjoyed making plants grow. People still visit his garden in Uppsala. He grew a wide range of plants in a small space. You do not need a lot of room for a garden. You can grow one in a glass jar.

Materials:
- a large glass jar with a lid
- small pebbles or stones
- potting soil
- small plants, such as moss, ferns, and seedlings
- a spray bottle filled with water

Procedure:
1. Place the jar on its side and put in a layer of stones.
2. Cover the stones with soil.
3. Place your plants in the soil, pressing the soil down firmly.
4. Squirt enough water into the jar to dampen the soil.
5. Put on the lid and place the jar where it is warm and light, but not in direct sunlight.

You can enjoy your jar garden without giving it much attention. The plants drink the water and release it into the air. The water droplets then rain back down into the soil.

A Seed Collection

Flowering plants produce seeds, which make sure there is a next generation. You can make a seed collection. Look outdoors and find dandelion seeds. Pine cones have seeds in them. You can also collect seeds in your own kitchen or on your dinner plate. An ear of corn has corn seeds. Beans are bean seeds. Look for seeds inside lemons, oranges, plums, cucumbers, avocados, and tomatoes.

Botany books often provide a key to help you find the name of a flower. Using a plant key is like going on a treasure hunt. You have to follow the clues. If you choose the right path, you learn the name of the flower.

Try making your own key to seeds you might find in your kitchen. Decide what characters to use to separate them. You could separate the seeds of avocado, plum, bean, corn, orange, lemon, tomato, and cucumber like this:

1. Seeds that are on their own. Go to 2
 Seeds that like company.   Go to 3

2. Diameter greater than a quarter: Avocado
 Diameter less than a quarter: Plum

3. Seeds that grow in a pod: Bean
 Seeds without a pod.   Go to 4

4. Seeds in a fleshy or juicy fruit. Go to 5
 Seeds sticking to a hard core: Corn

5. Fruit divided into segments: Orange
             Lemon

Fruit not in segments: Tomato
             Cucumber

Once you have made a key, have a friend try it out to see how well it works.

Classification

The trees in the woods, the flowers in the fields, and the bugs in your garden have already been given names. Linnaeus and a lot of other scientists got there first. What if it were up to you? What would you name an oak tree? Or a dandelion? Or a firefly? What flower or bug would you name in honor of your best friend?

Some Examples of Binomial Nomenclature

TODAY, SCIENTISTS STILL USE LINNAEUS'S SYSTEM OF BINOMIAL nomenclature, but they have introduced some new groupings. The most common divisions are (from largest to smallest): Kingdom, Phylum, Class, Order, Family, Genus, Species. Most scientists now recognize five Kingdoms: Animals, Plants, Fungi (mushrooms and funguses), Protists (microscopic living things), and Monerans (bacteria and blue-green algae). Following are the scientific names (genus and species) of some familiar plants and animals.

In this and all texts, a name followed by "L." indicates a species named by Linnaeus. Sometimes names are changed to fit with new ideas. The "L." is then put in parentheses, followed by the name of the scientist who has made the change. For example, Linnaeus originally described the orange as being in another genus. Osbeck later moved it to the genus *Citrus*, where it is today. So it is listed as "*Citrus sinensis* (L.) Osbeck." Linnaeus named the domestic cat *Felis catus* (cat cat) but it is now *Felis domesticus*. Occasionally, Linnaeus's sense of humor comes through in his choice of names. He had a hard time separating very small creatures into distinct species. He settled on the name of *Chaos chaos* for a one-celled amoeba! Read the names on the next page and think about why Linnaeus might have chosen these names.

Some Examples of Binomial Nomenclature

PLANTS		
Common Name	**Species Name**	**Literal Meaning**
Banana	*Musa paradisiaca* L.	fruit of paradise
Broccoli	*Brassica oleracea* L.	cabbage, smelly
Buttercup	*Ranunculus acris* L.	little frog, bitter
Crimson clover	*Tnfolium incarnata* L.	three leaves, blood red
Cucumber	*Cucumis sativus* L.	cucumber, cultivated
Dog rose	*Rosa canina* L.	rose, dog
Marijuana	*Cannabis sativa* L.	hemp, cultivated
Orange	*Citrus sinensis* (L.) Osbeck	citron, Chinese
Pea	*Pisum sativus* L.	pea, cultivated
Poison ivy	*Rhus toxicodendron* L.	sumac, poison leaves
Potato	*Solanum tuberosa* L.	nightshade, tubers
Sunflower	*Helianthus annuus* L.	sunflower, annual
Rice	*Oryza sativa* L.	rice, cultivated
Tobacco	*Nicotiana tabacum* L.	Nicot's tobacco
Twinflower	*Linnea borealis* L.	Linnaeus, northern
White clover	*Trifolium repens* L.	three leaves, creeping
White pine	*Pinus strobus* L.	pine, pinecone

ANIMALS		
Common Name	**Species Name**	**Literal Meaning**
Blue whale	*Balaenoptera musculus* L.	whale-wing, little mouse
Cat	*Felis domesticus*	cat, domestic
Dog	*Canis familiaris* L.	hound, domestic
Elephant (African)	*Loxodonta africana*	slanted tooth, African
Elephant (Indian)	*Elephas maximus* L.	elephant, great
Frog	*Rana tigrina* L.	frog, tiger
Gray wolf	*Canis lupus* L.	hound, wolf
Harlequin duck	*Histrionicus histrionicus* L.	theatrical, theatrical
Honey bee	*Apis mellifera* L.	bee, honey-bearing
Horse	*Equus caballus* L.	horse, packhorse
House fly	*Musca domistica* L.	fly, house
House mouse	*Mus musculus* L.	mouse, little mouse
Human beings	*Homo sapiens* L.	human, wise
Merganser duck	*Mergus merganser* L.	seagull, diving
Moose	*Alces alces* L.	elk, elk
Robin (American)	*Turdus migratorius* L.	thrush, wanderer
Salmon (Atlantic)	*Salmo salar* L.	salmon, salty
Silkworm	*Bombyx mori* L.	silkworm, mulberry
Tyrannosaurus rex*	*Tyrannosaurus rex*	tyrant-lizard king
Wild Turkey	*Meleagris gallopavo* L.	Meleager's (a Greek hero whose sisters were turned into birds) peacock

*extinct

Chronology

1707—Carl Linnaeus is born in Râshult, Sweden, on May 23.

1717—Goes to school in Växjö.

1727—Enters Lund University.

1728—Transfers to Uppsala University.

1730—Gives botany lectures at Uppsala.

1732—Travels to Lapland.

1733—Linnaeus's mother, Christina Linnaea, dies.

1734—Leads expedition to Dalarna.

1735—Earns medical degree in Holland; *Systema Naturae* is published; friend and colleague Peter Artedi dies.

1736—Travels to England.

1738—*Hortus Cliffortianus* is published; Linnaeus returns to Sweden from Holland; becomes a doctor in Stockholm.

1739—Marries Sara Lisa Moraea; Linnaeus is one of the founders of the Royal Swedish Academy of Sciences.

1741—Son Carl is born; travels to Öland and Gotland; becomes professor of medicine at Uppsala University; *Öland and Gotland Journey* is published.

1742—Becomes professor of botany.

1743—Daughter Lisa Stina is born.

1748—Linnaeus's father, Nils Linnaeus, dies.

1749—Daughter Louisa is born.

1750—Linnaeus is appointed rector of Uppsala University for the first time; he will serve as rector again in 1759 and in 1772.

1751—Daughter Sara Stina is born.

1753—*Species Plantarum* is published.

1754—Son Johannes is born; he dies in 1757.

1757—Daughter Sophia is born.

1758—Buys Hammarby Estate; tenth edition of *Systema Naturae* is published.

1761—Raised to the nobility and changes name to von Linné.

1768—Twelfth edition of *Systema Naturae* is completed.

1778—Dies in Uppsala on January 10.

Chapter Notes

Chapter 1. A Passion for Names

1. Heinz Goerke, *Linnaeus* (New York: Charles Scribner's Sons, 1973), p. 95.

2. Surnames were not common in Sweden when Nils Linnaeus was a young man. When he started university, he needed a last name. He chose the Latin name Linnaeus in honor of an ancient linden tree that grew on the family farm. Linnaeus is the masculine Latin form. Carl Linnaeus's mother's name is Christina Linnaea. Linnaea is the feminine form of the name Linnaeus.

3. Goerke, p. 89.

4. Wilfrid Blunt, *Linnaeus: The Compleat Naturalist* (Princeton, N.J.: Princeton University Press, 2001), p. 13.

Chapter 2. The Reluctant Student

1. Heinz Goerke, *Linnaeus* (New York: Charles Scribner's Sons, 1973), p. 13.

2. Wilfrid Blunt, *Linnaeus: The Compleat Naturalist* (Princeton, N.J.: Princeton University Press, 2001), p. 16.

3. Goerke, p. 14.

Chapter 3. Uppsala University

1. Wilfrid Blunt, *Linnaeus: The Compleat Naturalist* (Princeton, N.J.: Princeton University Press, 2001), p. 28.

2. Ibid., p. 37.

Chapter 4. Lapland Adventure

1. Lisbet Koerner, *Linnaeus: Nature and Nation* (Cambridge, Mass.: Harvard University Press, 1999), p. 59.

2. Ibid., p. 60

3. Wilfrid Blunt, *Linnaeus: The Compleat Naturalist* (Princeton, N.J.: Princeton University Press, 2001), p. 50.

4. David Black, ed., *Carl Linnaeus Travels* (New York: Charles Scribner's Sons, 1979), p. 31.

5. Blunt, p. 58.

Chapter 5. Back in Uppsala

1. Wilfrid Blunt, *Linnaeus: The Compleat Naturalist* (Princeton and Oxford: Princeton University Press, 2001), p. 74.

Chapter 6. Clifford's Garden

1. Heinz Goerke, *Linnaeus* (New York: Charles Scribner's Sons, 1973), p. 96.

2. Wilfrid Blunt, *Linnaeus: The Compleat Naturalist* (Princeton, N.J.: Princeton University Press, 2001), p. 101.

Chapter 7. The New Doctor

1. Wilfrid Blunt, *Linnaeus: The Compleat Naturalist* (Princeton, N.J.: Princeton University Press, 2001), p. 130.

2. Ibid.

3. Ibid., p. 136.

4. Carl Linnaeus, *Öland and Gotland Journey 1741* (London: Academic Press, 1973), pp. 78–79.

5. Blunt, p. 145.

Chapter 8. The Professor

1. Wilfrid Blunt, *Linnaeus: The Compleat Naturalist* (Princeton, N.J.: Princeton University Press, 2001), p. 150.

2. Ibid., p. 156.
3. Ibid., p. 177.
4. Ibid., p. 171.

Chapter 9. The Apostles
1. Heinz Goerke, *Linnaeus* (New York: Charles Scribner's Sons, 1973), p. 151.
2. Wilfrid Blunt, *Linnaeus: The Compleat Naturalist* (Princeton, N.J.: Princeton University Press, 2001), p. 188.
3. Ibid., p. 189.
4. Ibid., p. 191.
5. James Edward Smith, *A Selection of the Correspondence of Linnaeus and Other Naturalists* (New York: Arno Press, 1978), vol. 1, p. 222.

Chapter 10. Prince of Botanists
1. Wilfrid Blunt, *Linnaeus: The Compleat Naturalist* (Princeton, N.J.: Princeton University Press, 2001), p. 199.
2. Ibid., p. 230.
3. Ibid., p. 237.

Chapter 11. Before and After Linnaeus
1. Aristotle, *On the Parts of Animals*, trans. James G. Lennox (New York: Oxford University Press, 2001), pp. 8–9.
2. Wilfrid Blunt, *Linnaeus: The Compleat Naturalist* (Princeton, N.J.: Princeton University Press, 2001), p. 130.
3. Charles Darwin, *The Autobiography of Charles Darwin and Selected Letters*, ed. Francis Darwin (Mineola, N.Y.: Dover Publications, Inc., 1958), p. 184.

Activities
1. Florence Caddy, *Through the Fields With Linnaeus* (London: Longmans, Green, and Co., 1887), p. 20.

Glossary

anther—The head of the flower's stamen, it bears the pollen.

binomial system of nomenclature—Two-word method of naming.

clade—A group of organisms that share a common ancestor.

cladistics—A method of classification based on relationships.

dean—The head of a cathedral, or of a college at a university.

DNA—Stores the code for inherited characteristics. DNA stands for deoxyribonucleic acid.

filament—The long, thin part of the stamen that holds up the anther.

genus (pl. genera)—The grouping of a species.

gibbet—The gallows; where someone is hanged.

herbarium—A collection of pressed and dried plants.

lichen—A type of plant that is made up of an alga and a fungus growing together.

mussel—A type of shellfish.

orangery—A greenhouse used especially for growing oranges in colder regions.

order—A major division in classification; orders are divided into families, genera, and species.

ovary—The sac at the bottom of the pistil that holds the ovules.

ovule—The part of the plant that becomes a seed when it is fertilized by pollen.

pistil—The female part of a flower; it is made up of the stigma, style, and ovary.

pollination—The transfer of pollen from the anther to the stigma.

species—A group of organisms that closely resemble one another and are able to inter-breed.

stamen—The male part of a flower consisting of an anther and a filament.

stigma—The opening at the tip of a plant's pistil, it receives the pollen.

style—The tube that connects the stigma to the ovary.

taxonomy—The science of classification.

Further Reading

Cullen, Katherine. *Biology: The People Behind the Science*. New York: Chelsea House, 2006.

Kelsey, Elin. *Strange New Species: Astonishing Discoveries of Life on Earth*. Toronto: Maple Tree Press, 2005.

Stefoff, Rebecca. *The Flowering Plant Division*. New York: Marshall Cavendish Benchmark, 2006.

Stefoff, Rebecca. *The Primate Order*. New York: Marshall Cavendish Benchmark, 2006.

Internet Addresses

The Linnean Society of London
http://www.linnean.org/

Carl Linnaeus Biography,
    British Natural History Museum
http://www.nhm.ac.uk
    In the search area, type in 'Carl Linnaeus'

The Linnaeus Garden, Uppsala University
http://www.linnaeus.uu.se/LTeng.html

Index

nutrition, 72

O

Öland, 4, 41, 66–70, 117
order, 31, 53, 114, 122
Osbeck, Peter, 83–84, 114

P

pastor, 11, 14, 16–20, 38,
    49, 82
pearl, 42, 88, 90
pistil, 29–31, 54, 99, 123
Pitea, 41–42
pollen, 101
pollination, 29, 122

Q

Queen Ulrika, 62, 72, 83,
    88

R

Råshult, 10–11, 117
Ray, John, 9, 98
reindeer, 34, 37–38, 40
Rosén, Nils, 26, 33, 44,
    64, 71, 91
Rothman, Johan, 16–19,
    25, 66
Rudbeck, Olaf, 26, 30–33,
    64, 71, 115
Russia, 12, 41, 70

S

Smith, James Edward,
    95–96
Sohlberg, Claes, 46, 49–52
Solander, Daniel, 85,
species, 4, 7, 9, 44, 53, 58,
    72, 77, 83, 97, 99–102,

105–106, 114–116, 119,
    122–123
Species Plantarum, 77, 83,
    118
stamen, 9, 29, 30–31,
    53–54, 99, 122–123
Stenbrohult, 4, 11, 21–22,
    25, 33, 41, 45, 60
Stobaeus, Dr., 21, 23–24, 27
Stockholm, 12, 41, 61–62,
    64–65, 90, 117
Systema Naturae, 52–53, 78,
    117–119

T

Tärnström, Christopher, 82
taxonomist, 9, 100–102,
    106
taxonomy, 9, 101, 123
Tessin, Count Carl, 62
Thunberg, Carl, 86
Tournefort, Joseph, 9, 19,
    21, 98
twinflower, 10, 84, 115

U

Umeå, 4, 35, 37, 40–41
Uppsala, 12, 25–29, 32–33,
    41, 45–48, 56–57, 64,
    66, 71, 73, 78, 81, 87,
    90, 93–95, 111, 117–119

V

Växjö, 5, 14, 16–17, 41,
    66, 117

Z

zoology, 26